LESSONS

FROM OUR

ANCESTORS

by
Raksha Dave

illustrated by
Kimberlie Clinthorne-Wong

MAGIC CAT 🐾 PUBLISHING

To my mum and sisters, and to Nigel, Ruben, Elliot and Asha who have patiently spent the past two years listening to my 'interesting facts' at the dinner table – **R.D.**

To my mom and dad, with all my love. Thank you for all your love, support and encouragement. Hugs! – **K.C.W.**

MAGIC CAT PUBLISHING

First published in 2023 by Magic Cat Publishing, an imprint of Lucky Cat Publishing Ltd,
Unit 2 Empress Works, 24 Grove Passage, London E2 9FQ, UK

A catalogue record for this book is available from the British Library.

ISBN 978-1-913520-94-6

The illustrations were created digitally
Set in Balthazar, Active and Killer Elephant

Published by Rachel Williams and Jenny Broom
Designed by Stephanie Jones and Ella Tomkins
Edited by Helen Brown

Manufactured in China

9 8 7 6 5 4 3 2 1

FSC
www.fsc.org
MIX
Paper | Supporting responsible forestry
FSC® C104723

CONTENTS

Every object tells a story.

Archaeology is the study of people through the evidence they have left behind, from buildings and tools to bones and teeth. Linking all these things is like doing a jigsaw puzzle, helping archaeologists like me to recreate how people in the past lived. You might think archaeologists are only interested in precious objects such as jewellery or coins, but often the most common everyday items, like bricks or food remains, can tell us so much more.

This book draws on fifty objects to offer a fresh perspective on people from our past who can teach lessons that are valuable to us today. You'll have already heard of formidable gladiators from ancient Rome, vicious Vikings from the Norse homelands and a pharaoh called Tutankhamun who ruled over Egypt, but what about the ancient city in Turkey where gender equality flourished, the benevolent king from India who cared for the disadvantaged, or the Inca citadel that was built on migration?

We're going to travel back in time to fourteen civilisations and cast a spotlight on forgotten histories and misrepresented stories. We'll celebrate equality, inclusivity and sustainability across the ancient world, and I hope that by learning important lessons from our ancestors you will feel inspired to build a better future.

After all, what legacy will you leave for future archaeologists to uncover?

Raksha Dave

Archaeologist and broadcaster

AUSTRALIA'S FIRST PEOPLES WERE CONSERVATIONISTS

WHEN
Around 40,000 BCE

WHERE
Lake Mungo, Australia

Australia is home to the oldest continuous culture on Earth – a culture which protects and preserves the environment.

Over forty thousand years ago, the first peoples of Australia sailed across the ocean from Asia to settle in Australia. At a time when most of the world was locked in ice, the ancestors of the Paakantji, Mutthi Mutthi and Ngiyampaa thrived. All three groups came together at Lake Mungo and the Willandra Lakes region, and just as the land looked after them, they in turn cared for the land. This is still the case today, as the Paakantji, Mutthi Mutthi and Ngiyampaa people continue their close connections to the land at Lake Mungo, and the fact that their cultures have thrived for so long is a testament to their sustainability.

The ancestors of the Paakantji, Mutthi Mutthi and Ngiyampaa were **CARETAKERS** of the environment. They protected their land, respected wildlife and made use of knowledge passed down through the generations.

FIRE PITS were dug with digging sticks and were made for the same reasons that people use them today – to cook food and keep warm. They were built in a variety of ways: using charcoal, creating clay fireplaces and even from the caps of termites' nests.

Dome-shaped tents, known as **GUNYAHS**, were built from sticks, bark, and sometimes, leaves. They were cleverly dotted along the lake's shoreline to be in the best position to gather food.

Indigenous Australians left behind the oldest **FOOTPRINTS** ever found in Australia. Tracks tell amazing stories, like the fact that foragers included all members of a group: women, men… and even children!

Although they were limited to foods occurring naturally in their area, the ancestors of the Paakantji, Mutthi Mutthi and Ngiyampaa knew exactly when, where and how to find everything edible. They hunted for fish like perch and Murray cod using **HAND-HELD NETS** made of woven plant fibres.

THE OBJECTS THAT REVEAL Lake Mungo's STORY

Footprints

Approximately five hundred ancient footprints have been recorded in the claypans at Lake Mungo. These footprints are the oldest found in Australia, and the world's largest set of Ice Age footprints. They unearth a story of how humans have visited, foraged, hunted and lived around Lake Mungo for millennia.

When the footprints were uncovered, Mary Pappin, a Mutthi Mutthi elder, said walking alongside the footprints was like 'walking with a family group today. They're the same people.' She believed the prints had been revealed 'to let the rest of the world know how clever our people really were, living and surviving in their environment'.

This net is one of the oldest fishing tools in the world.

Fishing nets

By weaving together **PLANTS** which grew around the lake's edge, hand-held fishing nets were constructed at Lake Mungo. Plant fibres were stripped into pieces, twisted into yarn and laced together to create a **TIGHT WEBBING** to catch passing fish.

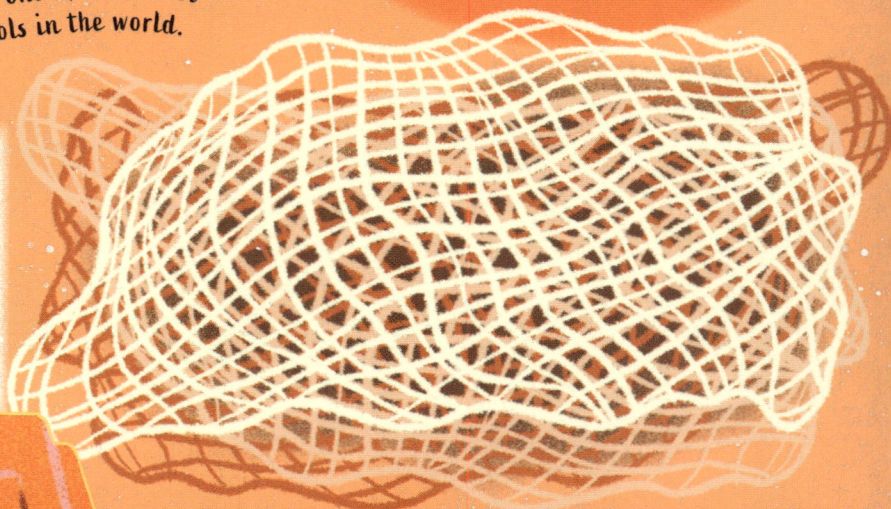

MUNGO MAN

In 1974, a geologist discovered 'Mungo Man' – the oldest-known human remains in Australia. After the body was excavated, Mungo Man's bones were lifted from their burial place and taken to the National Museum of Australia in Canberra. This caused great distress to Mungo Man's descendants as they were not consulted nor asked for permission for the remains to be removed.

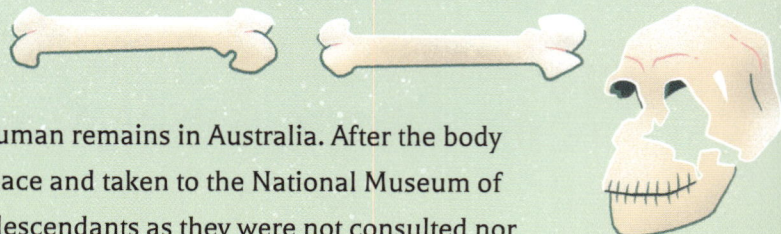

Middens

Middens are the remains of **MEALS** (similar to a rubbish pile) which can tell archaeologists about the diet of people from the past. The bones and shells found in the middens at Lake Mungo reveal that the ancestors of the Paakantji, Mutthi Mutthi and Ngiyampaa were eating **FRESHWATER ANIMALS**, including perch, Murray cod, mussels and crayfish.

Archaeologists can tell that these middens belonged to people because they were arranged in ways that could not have occurred naturally.

Grindstones

Grindstones were essential for turning seeds into flour for **BAKING BREAD**. The earliest civilisations in Jordan were once thought to be the first bakers, but it was actually Indigenous Australians who started the practice almost ten thousand years previously. Stone wasn't easy to find around Lake Mungo, and so this precious resource was likely to have been traded or collected, showing us an incredibly early form of **BARTERING**.

Mungo Man was returned home in 2017 after decades of campaigning – and was welcomed back in an emotional ceremony of dance and song. The story serves to remind archaeologists to always consider the rights of the deceased, their relatives and the community to which they belong. Today, archaeologists stick to a code of ethics: a list of rules to make sure that human remains are respected and treated with dignity.

WOMEN AND CHILDREN PAINTED THE CHAUVET CAVE

One of the oldest artwork in history was created by women and children.

More than thirty thousand years ago, a group of nomadic people called the Aurignacians travelled for miles following migrating herds for food. They were hunters, but they were also artists. They created paintings on the walls of Chauvet Cave, drawing animals from horses to woolly mammoths! It was thought that their art commemorated their kills, which is why historians assumed that the artists must have been male because they believed only men were hunter-gatherers. Actually, most of the art created in Europe at this time was crafted by women and children – making them the true artists of some of the earliest masterpieces in the world.

Women and children used two main colours to create their cave art: red and black. These colours were natural materials known as **PIGMENTS**.

Wood from Scots pines (a species of tree) was burned to create a soft, black, charred lump known as charcoal to create a **PREHISTORIC PENCIL**.

Alongside their artistic work, Aurignacian women were **BIG-GAME HUNTERS**. Hunting was important for survival and so participation from everyone in the group made good evolutionary sense for many hunter-gatherer groups.

HAND ART was made by placing a palm covered with pigment on the wall, or by putting a hand against the wall and using the mouth to blow pigment around it to form a stencil.

Artists learned to make small, sharp **TOOLS** from stone, antler, bone or wood. These tools were used to create incisions on the hard limestone walls.

THE OBJECTS THAT REVEAL THE Chauvet Cave's STORY

Animal art

Herds of **HERBIVORES** were a common theme in Stone Age art, but predatory animals were featured, too. They were painted with incredible attention to muscular detail, and some researchers proposed that this work was created by men because they followed the stereotypical view of a **GENDERED DIVISION OF LABOUR** in hunter-gatherer groups, with men hunting and women staying at home. However, recent studies have shown that men weren't the only hunters in Palaeolithic families, and it is likely that women and teenage children took part in hunting, too.

Fire pits

Crystallised ashes from an ancient fire pit tell us that the black drawings in the Chauvet Cave were made by applying **CHARCOAL**. This charcoal was made by burning wood or other organic matter in fire pits, and these pits were occasionally surrounded by limestone to show other artists where established fire pits existed. This helped them to make their next batch of charcoal, showing a **HARMONY** between clans.

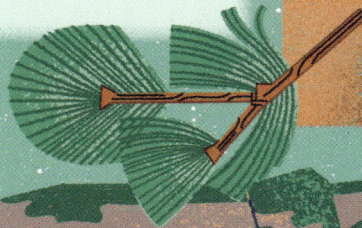

CONSERVATION IN ACTION

Three cave explorers stumbled upon the Chauvet Cave in December 1994 and it became one of the biggest discoveries of the twentieth century. The entrance to the cave had been sealed by an ancient rockfall for millennia, and the air within the cave had stayed the same for more than twenty thousand years. Just like screwing a lid onto a jam jar, the contents inside had been perfectly preserved.

Hand art

Hundreds of prints cover the walls of Chauvet – an incredible signature left behind by the artists of the vivid prehistoric artwork found within. Each piece of **HAND ART** was made using **PIGMENTS**, and from analyses of cave-painting materials, it appears that these pigments were made into a powder by grinding, then mixed with a binder such as plant sap which acted a bit like glue.

At least 75 per cent of the handprints analysed from all Palaeolithic caves in France belonged to women or children, overturning the idea that Europe's first artists were men. We know this because archaeologists measured the size and finger lengths of each hand. Women mostly have ring and index fingers of about the same length, whereas men's ring fingers tend to be longer than their index fingers.

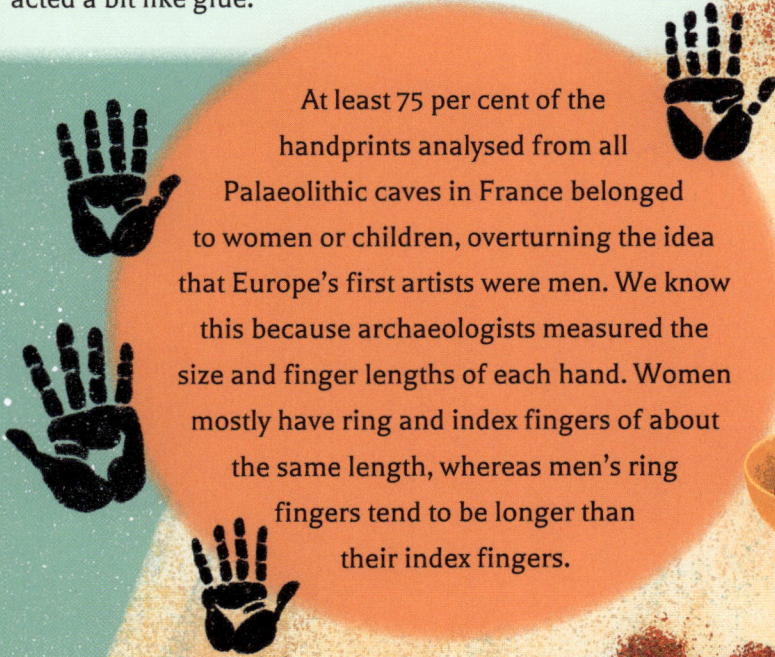

Chauvet Cave contains 12 red ochre handprints, 9 hand stencils and 450 palm prints.

Abstract art

Some of the world's **EARLIEST ABSTRACT ART** and **TECHNIQUES** can be seen inside Chauvet. For these Palaeolithic artists the making of abstract designs is of equal importance to the realistic drawings they created. The techniques that they employed range from the earliest use of shading, **POINTILLISM** (small, distinct dots of colour applied in patterns to form an image) and hand stencilling.

Today the cave is closed to visitors as their presence would likely destroy the fragile atmosphere – the carbon dioxide released from people's breath would encourage bacteria to form and destroy these priceless pieces of art. Only a handful of scientists, conservators and researchers are allowed to visit the cave each year, where they monitor the environment, protect the paintings and share the stories of Chauvet and its prehistoric artists with the rest of the world.

GENDER EQUALITY BLOSSOMED IN ÇATALHÖYÜK

There were equal rights for men and women in the ancient city of Çatalhöyük.

You may think that gender equality is a modern concept, but around nine thousand years ago, groups of Neolithic and Chalcolithic hunter-gatherers abandoned their nomadic lives and collectively built a society in Çatalhöyük where men and women held the same status. There weren't any elite ruling groups – like kings, queens or chiefs – nor any divisions based on gender. Day-to-day tasks, from farming to baking, were shared among different households and completed together cooperatively. Life continued at Çatalhöyük for 1,400 years, and it became the most populated, organised and settled city from the Neolithic and Chalcolithic periods.

Rectangular **MUDBRICK HOUSES** were similar in size and layout, showing an early type of urban design based on **COMMUNITY** and **EQUALITY**. Families built them close together and climbed over roofs to access rooms from above.

Men and women carried out the **SAME JOBS** and spent the same amount of time indoors and outdoors, from tending to the animals and making tools to baking and running a household.

QUERNSTONES (an ancient device for grinding grains like corn) and **COOKING POTS** were expensive to obtain and so were **SHARED EQUALLY** between households.

Children observed adults at **WORK**, learning how to perform rituals, create pieces of art, build houses and harvest food.

THE OBJECTS THAT REVEAL Çatalhöyük's STORY

Cooking pots

Remnants of food found in **COOKING POTS** reveal what the people of Çatalhöyük ate. Bread and porridge were regularly eaten, as was meat from cows, sheep and goats. Milk from these animals was also turned into **DAIRY PRODUCTS** such as cheese or yoghurt, making Çatalhöyük one of the oldest places in the world to have consumed and processed milk.

By examining wear on teeth, osteoarchaeologists (people who study the skeletal remains of humans found on archaeological sites) have discovered that both sexes ate the same diet. This is significant because if one or the other had a higher status then we might expect to uncover differences in diet – such as one group having more access to meat, which would have been of high value at the time.

Figurines

The people of Çatalhöyük made many different types of figurines out of **CLAY** and **STONE**. Effigies representing male, female and animal gods have been found, suggesting all three were **EQUALLY WORSHIPPED**.

EQUALITY IN EVERY WAY

Inspired by the people who lived there 9,000 years ago, the Çatalhöyük excavation worked in the way that the people of Çatalhöyük lived their lives: equally. The dig was unique as excavators and specialists lived together on site and gave everyone the same opportunity to collaborate and interpret the artefacts. Their thoughts and ideas flowed as they collectively unpicked the puzzles of the past.

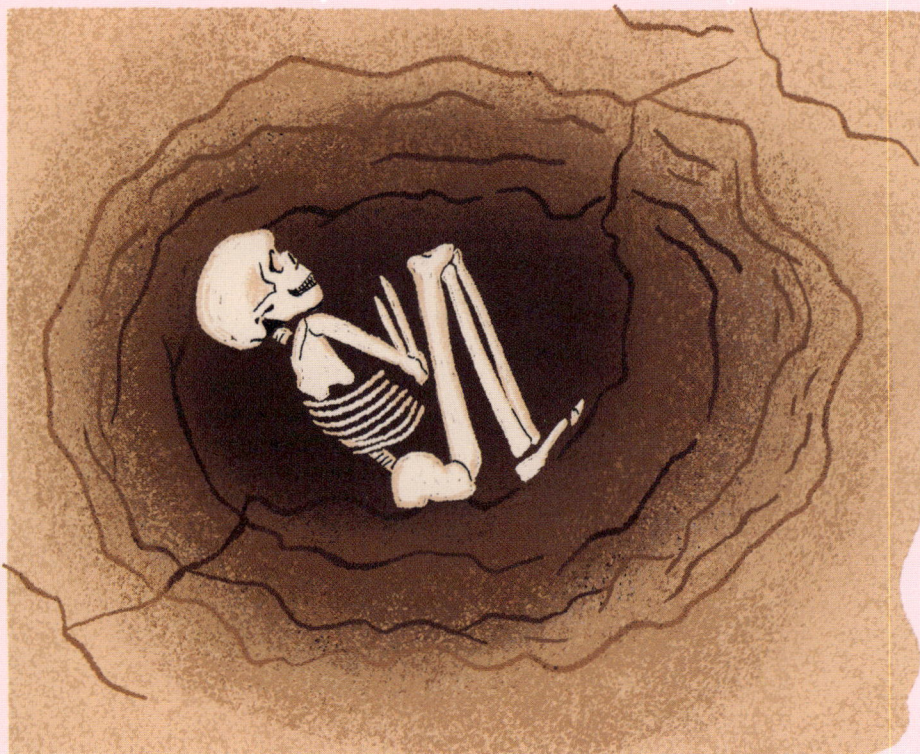

Human remains

Archaeologists discovered that there was no difference in the way the people of Çatalhöyük were buried: everyone was treated **EQUALLY IN LIFE AND DEATH**. Instead of using cemeteries, they buried their dead in pits dug underneath the main rooms of their houses. Bodies were bound in a curled-up **FOETAL POSITION**; some were placed in baskets, while others were wrapped in reeds or oak-fibre mats.

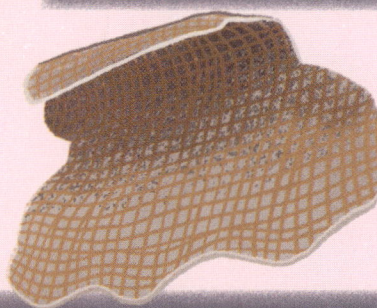

Ovens

Those who lived in Çatalhöyük resided in small houses, and ovens were generally placed on the south side of the main rooms. **IDENTICAL SOOT RESIDUES** from these ovens were found on the rib bones of the deceased, showing us that men and women lived similar lives in terms of the length of time spent inside the house as the same amount of soot got into people's lungs.

The responsibility of cooking was likely shared equally between men and women.

The team connected with surrounding villages; they asked local people to help with the excavation and provided a space for them to share stories about their landscape and traditions. To this day, the people living in the surrounding area use the same methods to make mudbricks as the people of Çatalhöyük did nine millennia ago, giving archaeologists an insight into the ways that modern people can be so deeply connected with their prehistoric ancestors.

MOHENJO-DARO WAS A SUSTAINABLE CITY

WHEN
Around 2500–1900 BCE

WHERE
Mohenjo-daro,
Pakistan

Mohenjo-daro was more sustainable than most cities today.

Imagine a sustainable city, planned entirely with the wellbeing of its citizens in mind. Where residents are cooled by air carefully designed to flow through its streets by day and are warmed by heat-retaining buildings by night. Where citizens drink crystal-clear rainwater and use waste to fertilise the crops, feeding its population year-round with organic produce. It sounds like something from the future, doesn't it? In fact, this is Mohenjo-daro, nestled on the fertile banks of the Indus River, an ancient city built by the Harappan civilisation around four and a half thousand years ago. Housing 40,000 people, Mohenjo-daro was equal in size to many well-known cities at the time. But unlike the societies of ancient Greece and Egypt, Mohenjo-daro was unique: it was self-sufficient in every way.

The people of Mohenjo-daro were skilled at **LIVING OFF THE LAND**. Jewellery made from unearthed seashells, pearls and beads were bought and sold at the thriving marketplace.

During monsoon season, **RAINWATER** filled the **700 WELLS** built around the city. It was collected and saved so everyone had access to water, even during dry spells.

Houses had **THICK WALLS** made of kiln-fired bricks. The light colour of the bricks reflected the heat from the sun, and the heat from the air was absorbed by the mass of the walls, keeping homes **COOL DURING THE DAY** and **WARM DURING THE NIGHT**.

The city had a brilliant underground **SEWAGE SYSTEM** that carried polluted water and waste out of homes... straight to farmers who used it as fertiliser to help their crops grow!

Mohenjo-daro was the first-known city to be constructed on a **GRID PLAN**, which meant streets ran at right angles to one another. This had social and economic benefits, allowing for more cultural exchanges and equality through shared blocks.

THE OBJECTS THAT REVEAL Mohenjo-daro's STORY

Beaded necklace

Made from gold and gemstones like agate and jasper, this intricate necklace was crafted by a skilled jeweller. **JEWELLERY-MAKING** was the main industry of the city and jewellery was made and worn by both men and women. Trade in these precious items brought **ECONOMIC WEALTH** and **SUSTAINABILITY** to Mohenjo-daro, contributing to the city's survival for hundreds of years.

Remnants of beads were found all over Mohenjo-daro – scattered next to kilns, hidden in pots for safekeeping or carelessly left by the side of the bath!

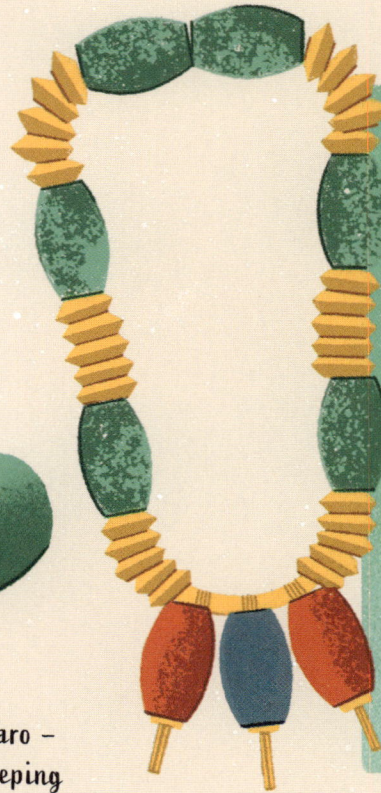

Limestone bricks

These bricks were part of an elaborately engineered **SEWAGE SYSTEM** which safely carried dirty water and waste away from Mohenjo-daro. The street drains were made of baked brick, and the bricks were closely fitted and sealed with mud mortar. Waste would enter terracotta pipes and travel through these street drains, each of which was connected to deeper limestone-built tunnels that **FLUSHED WASTE AWAY** from the city.

THE DECLINE OF MOHENJO-DARO

After 900 years of prosperous living, the people of Mohenjo-daro abandoned their sustainable city. What led to the decline of Mohenjo-daro and the Indus Valley civilisation as a whole is still a mystery. It was thought a foreign power conquered the city and forced people to leave their homes, but the archaeology suggests that it may have been a result of climate change causing a series of floods across the Indus Valley.

Cubic weights

Around five hundred and fifty stone cubic weights were excavated from Mohenjo-daro. It was these **WEIGHTS** and precise **MEASUREMENTS** that helped the Harappan people to build Mohenjo-daro with blocks divided by a grid of straight streets. One of the main benefits of the streets being laid out in a **PERPENDICULAR GRID** was airflow. Even though the city's climate was hot most of the year, the streets provided a comfortable cooling effect.

Mohenjo-daro had the world's first sewage system. It was mostly covered and hidden underground, just like ours is today.

Archaeologists used mattocks, trowels and shovels to unpick Mohenjo-daro's vast underground sewer system. They uncovered 300 manholes which serviced the sewage system and found evidence of 4,000-year-old waste still inside! City cleaners would open these regularly to collect the waste and pass it on to farmers, who would use it as fertiliser to help their crops grow.

A third theory suggests that increasing levels of salt in the water ruined crops and left lands infertile. This theory of the end of Mohenjo-daro is not dissimilar to the excavation site today. It is a complicated place to protect due to the levels of salt. The salt content in the groundwater is eating away at the bricks, and archaeologists are concerned that the ancient city from which we could learn so much from could soon be sadly lost forever.

WOMEN WARRIORS THRIVED IN ANCIENT CHINA

WHEN
Around 1600–1046 BCE

WHERE
Yinxu, China

Yinxu was home to the greatest military leader of the Shang dynasty: Fu Hao.

Over three and a half thousand years ago, ancient China was ruled by a powerful family of kings. This period was known as the Shang dynasty. A Shang monarch would rely on an army to protect their kingdom, and Fu Hao was an army general. She commanded 13,000 loyal soldiers, many of whom were women, too. She even overcame the mighty Tu Fang, an army that fought against the Shang for generations until it was finally defeated by Fu Hao and her army in a single battle! As time went on, the balance of power between men and women shifted, and Fu Hao's success descended into myth, with many historians unable to believe that a female military leader could ever have existed.

ORACLE BONES were used by army generals to seek advice on military strategy. Script was etched onto animal bones which were then heated until cracks appeared. Shang priests would then interpret the cracks and make predictions based on what they saw.

Fu Hao's army was equipped with an assortment of **BRONZE WEAPONRY** including spears, bows, helmets and yues (battle-axes). A battle-axe could slice a person in half with a single blow!

Alongside her military roles, Fu Hao became an active **POLITICIAN** and **INFLUENTIAL LEADER**. Both were unusual roles for women at the time.

Wooden boxes containing **COWRIE SHELLS** were seized from conquered lands. Used as a form of currency, cowries were given out to military leaders as a reward after successful battles.

THE OBJECTS THAT REVEAL Fu Hao's STORY

A total of 6,900 cowrie shells were found in Fu Hao's tomb.

Cowrie shells

Cowrie shells were used as a form of **CURRENCY** during the Shang dynasty, the same way we use coins today. The cowrie shells found in Fu Hao's tomb were from her personal fortune and captured during her **EPIC CONQUESTS**. Chinese inscriptions on bronze vessels dating to the Shang dynasty often refer to 'gifts of cowries', 'cowries in the treasury' or 'rewards of cowries' – suggesting that a percentage of these shells were distributed to generals as rewards after battles, with the larger share being given to the king and stored safely in his treasury.

Jade phoenix

The **PHOENIX** is a special symbol in Chinese mythology. It is thought that the Shang dynasty was founded by the descendants of a phoenix. Discovered in Fu Hao's tomb among her personal objects, jade effects like this phoenix were handed down as heirlooms – some thousands of years old and made by Neolithic ancestors. Fu Hao, who was equally celebrated as a **MILITARY GENERAL** and a **DEVOTED POLITICIAN**, was often described as 'hard as bronze and as soft as jade'.

THE TOMB OF FU HAO

Over the centuries that followed, Fu Hao's military accomplishments faded into legend. Until, in 1975, a team of Chinese archaeologists began examining land in the ancient city of Anyang, north-eastern China. Their job was to see if the area was clear of significant artefacts in order that be turned into agricultural fields, but to their surprise they discovered an intact royal tomb dating back to the Shang dynasty…

Bronze yues

Four bronze **AXE-SHAPED WEAPONS**, known as yues, were found in Fu Hao's tomb, in among 464 other bronze objects – a prominent display of her power and status as a military leader. Many of the bronze vessels were inscribed with her name, having often been used during battles or ceremonies.

The size of one yue weighed an impressive 9 kilograms!

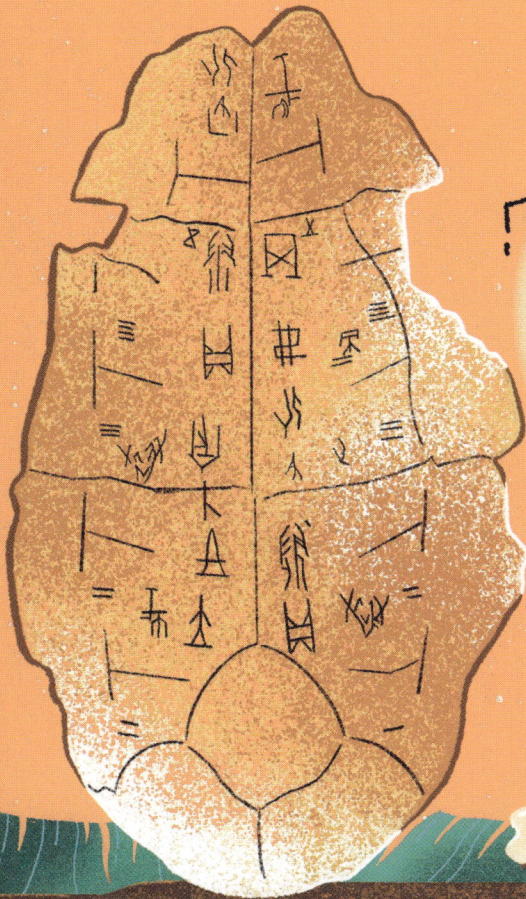

Oracle bones were used in an attempt to gain insight into a question or situation. The inscriptions are called pictographs, which is when an image depicts a word or phrase. They form the basis of some modern Chinese characters today.

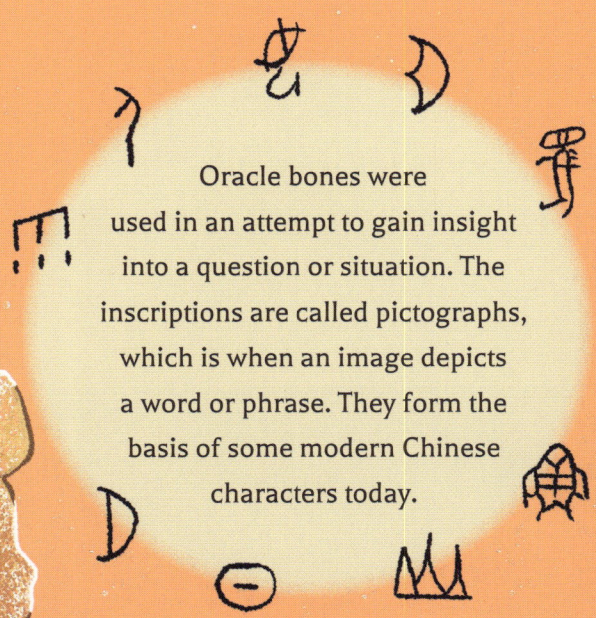

Oracle bones

FRAGMENTS of found oracle bones unlock Fu Hao's hidden history. One inscription read: 'It should be Fu Hao whom the king orders to campaign against Yi.' This gives us a rare glimpse into how much the **KING TRUSTED FU HAO** to lead his armies, go to battle against other soldiers on his behalf and win.

It quickly became clear that Fu Hao's final resting place was of great importance – the fact that a woman had been given such an elaborate burial tomb in ancient China was unusual, and it also contained hundreds of objects symbolic of a woman who held royal and military power. Twenty different types of bronze vessel were uncovered, seventy of which were inscribed with one name – Fu Hao – confirming the existence of China's first female military leader.

BLACK PHARAOHS RULED ANCIENT EGYPT

WHEN
747–656 BCE

WHERE
Nuri, modern Sudan

The Black Pharaohs were an ancient superpower that dominated the Nile Valley and rivalled the Egyptians.

The Black Pharaohs, also known as the Kings of the Kush Empire, ruled Egypt for 100 years. Taharqa was the most powerful emperor of the ancient world. He ruled for twenty-six years, and his land was rich in gold. During his reign, Taharqa restored existing pyramids and built new ones, and for almost three thousand years these pyramids were the only clues left of the mighty Kush kingdom. The Black Pharaohs' reign became legendary among African people, but was written off as hearsay by some racist historians who thought the Kush people couldn't build pyramids worthy of the same attention and respect as the Egyptians.

Kushite men and women were fierce warriors. Known for their skills with a bow and arrow, **ARCHERS** formed the core of Kush armies prompting the ancient Egyptians to name Kush 'Ta-Seti', meaning 'Land of the Bow'.

KUSH QUEENS were seen as equals to pharaohs, and often held important religious and political roles.

Around **255 KUSH PYRAMIDS** were built – compared with about 118 Egyptian ones! The Kush pyramids were erected using **SHADOOFS** (wooden counterweight cranes) and mathematical equations like **TRIGONOMETRY**.

When he became pharaoh, **TAHARQA** vowed to build pyramids – places where statues dedicated to important **GODS** lived. He hoped these statues would provide him with help in ruling over such a large kingdom.

The Kingdom of Kush's gold and ivory was prized throughout the Mediterranean and the Middle East, and sales of **PRECIOUS ITEMS** such as animal skins and ostrich feathers flourished under Taharqa's reign.

THE OBJECTS THAT REVEAL THE Black Pharaohs' STORY

Statue of Taharqa

A **STATUE OF TAHARQA** was uncovered alongside six fellow Black Pharaohs. We know which statue is Taharqa because his name appears on the centre of his belt, above his pleated kilt. Taharqa wears a headdress with double uraeus (two cobras) signifying his **POWERFUL RULE OVER TWO KINGDOMS**: Kush and Egypt.

Standing at an impressive height of 2.7 metres, Taharqa's size is a display of dominance.

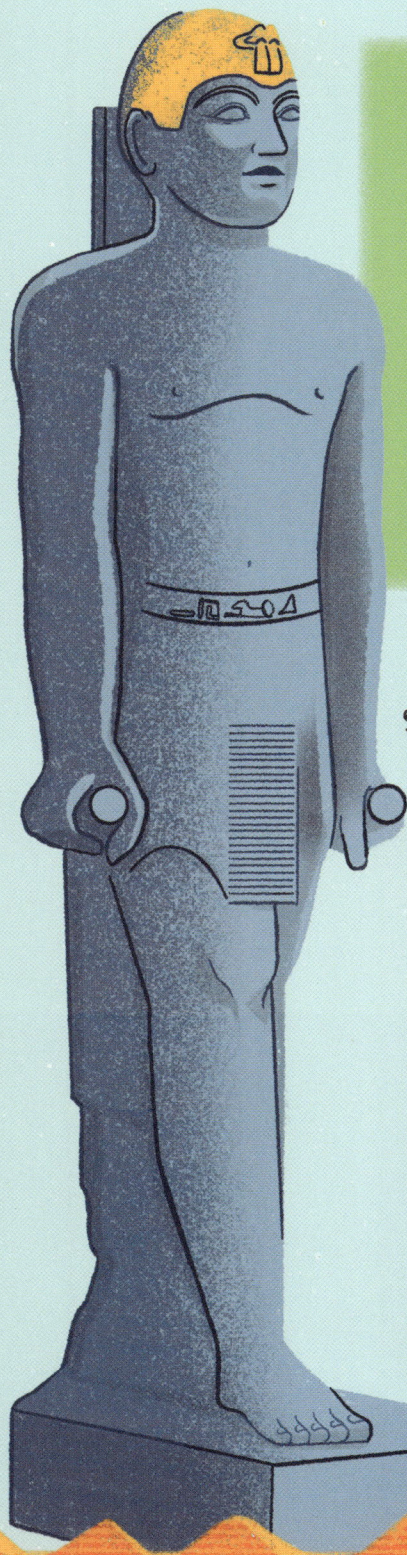

Statue of Amun-Re

This imposing granite statue was built by Taharqa. The ram represents **AMUN-RE**, the god of sun and air, with Taharqa standing below. Throughout his reign in Egypt, Taharqa used the symbolic imagery of Amun-Re to evoke power and strength, and many depictions of him show him wearing a ram's head and sun disc as a nod to Amun-Re.

RACE AGAINST TIME

For millennia, Kush sites like Nuri have been long forgotten. Recent discoveries and balanced perspectives now reshape the ways this civilisation's past is understood, and evidence is now emerging about how much this African kingdom contributed to the development of art, technology and construction, along with its influence on neighbouring civilisations in Egypt, Assyria and Greece.

Painting of Queen Yeturow

Fifty-three queens were buried in the **NURI PYRAMIDS**, and the most impressive tomb belonged to **QUEEN YETUROW**, the daughter of Taharqa. Kush queens were seen as equals to the king and were offered the same burials. In some cases, Kush queens would rule if a male relative had died.

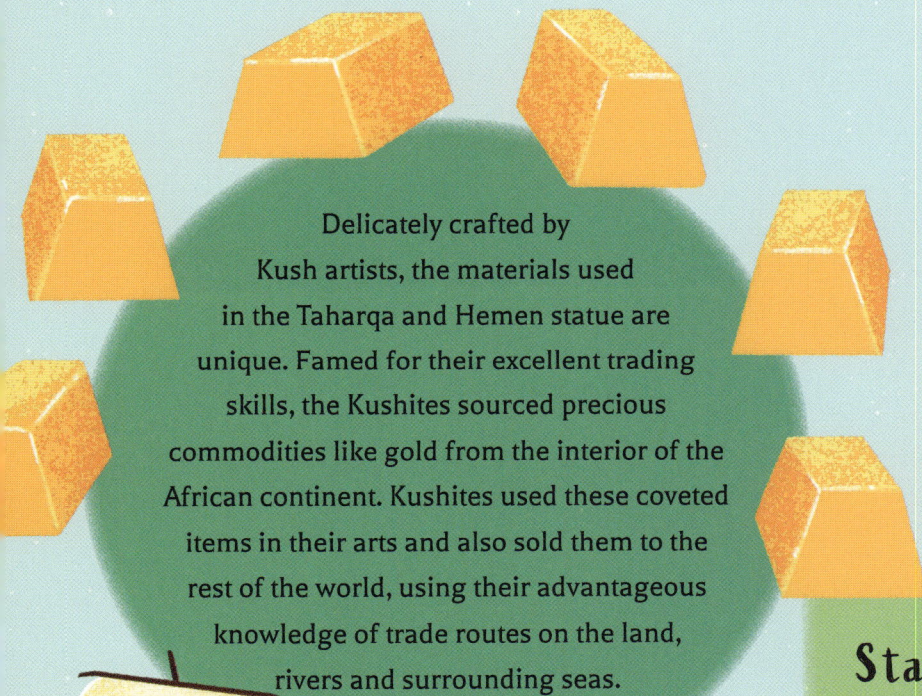

Delicately crafted by Kush artists, the materials used in the Taharqa and Hemen statue are unique. Famed for their excellent trading skills, the Kushites sourced precious commodities like gold from the interior of the African continent. Kushites used these coveted items in their arts and also sold them to the rest of the world, using their advantageous knowledge of trade routes on the land, rivers and surrounding seas.

Statue of Taharqa and Hemen

Five **MATERIALS** were used to create this statue of Taharqa and Hemen: gold, bronze, silver, stone and wood. Here, Taharqa kneels in worship before the **FALCON-GOD HEMEN**, who clutches a cobra in his talons – symbolic of Egypt and Nubia – and in return he offers Taharqa his protection.

However, there was a risk that the Kingdom of Kush would be lost forever due to the threat of climate change. When an archaeological expedition began work in 2018, extreme rainfall was found to have damaged the crumbling pyramids. The flooded tombs had been ravaged by time, but archaeologists found new ways to enter them (including diving underwater!) to help recover the true story of the Black Pharaohs before they disappeared into the desert for good.

WOMEN TRIUMPHED AT THE ANCIENT OLYMPIC GAMES

WHEN
396 BCE

WHERE
Olympia,
Greece

Kyniska was the first woman to compete in the 'male-only' ancient Olympic Games... and she won!

The Games that we see on television today have their origins in Ancient Greece, beginning almost three thousand years ago in Olympia. Every four years, men and boys entered competitions like the four-horse chariot race, but women and girls were not allowed to participate. However, they could train horses, and in the chariot race the trainers were also seen as winners – a loophole that Kyniska took advantage of. She coached a driver to victory, earning the first wreath ever bestowed on a woman. The fact that Kyniska didn't physically compete has led history to overlook her achievement, but her success inspired many women at the time who went on to attain similar greatness.

As the rules banned women from physically attending the Games, nobody knows for sure whether **KYNISKA** saw her horses win, although she may have been **SPECTATING** in the crowd, chaperoned by her brother.

FAST MESSENGERS carried word of an Olympic victory to the winner's home city, where celebratory preparations began at once, and news that a woman had won would have spread very quickly indeed!

Winning drivers received **WOOLLEN BANDS** to tie around their head, and trainers were crowned with an **OLIVE WREATH** and sometimes given a jar of **OLIVE OIL**, which was an extravagant prize at the time.

The four-horse chariots raced **TWELVE TIMES** around a track measuring about 8 miles. It was the most popular sport in ancient Greece, appealing to all **SOCIAL CLASSES**.

THE OBJECTS THAT REVEAL Kyniska's STORY

Kyniska's statue

Olympic winners celebrated their victories by getting famous Greek sculptors to make statues of their win. Inscribed on the base of Kyniska's statue was a **DECLARATION** that she was the **FIRST WOMAN** to win the wreath in the chariot race at the Olympic Games:

I, Kyniska, victorious with a chariot of swift-footed horses, have erected this statue. I declare myself the only woman in all Hellas to have won this crown.

Kyniska celebrated her **TRAILBLAZING VICTORY** boldly and proudly, and shared this message with women across Greek society.

Kyniska's stone statue base is now housed in the Museum of the Olympic Games in Greece.

'Epigraphy' is the study of engraved writing on various surfaces including stone. Stone writings can become damaged or fade over time by the weather, or pollution in the air or soil. Thankfully, due to technologies like X-ray fluorescence, archaeologists can recover faded text, allowing us to decipher stories left on ancient stone.

FROM ANCIENT TIMES TO MODERN TIMES

The ancient Olympic Games were held in Greece for over a thousand years, but they started to lose their importance when the Romans took over Greece in the second century BCE. At first the Romans continued to organise the Games, but in 394 CE Emperor Theodosius of Rome officially banned them. He followed the teachings of Christianity and wanted to put an end to any pagan festivals.

Amphora vases

Amphora vases were often filled with **OLIVE OIL** and were given as prizes to winners of the Games. Figures painted on the body of amphora vases show the variety of events athletes competed in. Kyniska's four-horse chariot race, also known as the **TETHRIPPON**, was one of the **OLDEST EVENTS** – and according to legend, when Pelops, the grandson of Zeus, defeated and killed King Oenomaus in a chariot race, he founded the games in honour of his victory.

Woollen band

VALUABLE PRIZES could be won in athletic contests all over the Greek world, but victory at Olympia brought the greatest prestige. Olympic winners tied this **WOOLLEN RED BAND** around their forehead, and sometimes around their arms and legs, as sign of victory. These ribbons have been represented on drinking cups, or **KYLIX**, and were given to the winners immediately after their win.

One thousand five hundred years later, the first modern Olympic Games took place in Athens in 1896, but women were still banned from competing. Over time, however, the Games gradually encouraged gender equality, as women and girls were able to compete in more and more events. At Tokyo 2020 (held in summer 2021) almost 49 per cent of the 11,000 athletes were women, making it the first 'gender-balanced' Games in Olympic history.

ASHOKA WAS A GREAT AND COMPASSIONATE KING

WHEN
Around 268–232 BCE

WHERE
Sarnarth, India

Emperor Ashoka preached messages of tolerance and compassion throughout his kingdom.

Taking a stroll through the ancient walkways of Sarnath, it may have dawned on you that this was a city with a difference. Public messages of inclusivity were placed prominently. Clean water was freely available, and crops were grown to provide food for everyone. Places of healing offered care to all citizens no matter their creed or status. The welfare of animals was promoted throughout the land. Looking after the city was a man considered to be one of the greatest Indian emperors of all time: Ashoka. His rule was influenced by his Buddhist faith, a new religion and philosophy founded by Siddhartha Gautama 'the Buddha', which saw Ashoka embark upon a pilgrimage across India to promote peace.

ASHOKA performed many acts of **SOCIAL WELFARE** during his pilgrimage. He established large hospitals and built freshwater wells. He even banned war, explaining there would only be 'conquest by Dharma' – a Buddhist moral code for the right life.

Dams were constructed to ensure a steady source of clean water reached towns and villages across India. **WATER CHANNELS** were diverted to fields so that enough crops were grown to provide food for all residents.

HOSPITALS were built for humans and animals, and care was available to everyone for free. Medicines were made using plants with healing properties which were grown nearby.

STONE PILLARS were erected across the Mauryan Empire, located in public places so everyone had access to them. Inscriptions called **EDICTS** were carved on them, and also on rocks too, to remind people to embrace **PEACEFUL LIVES**.

THE OBJECTS THAT REVEAL Ashoka's STORY

The lion is traditionally a symbol of royalty and leadership, and may represent Ashoka who ordered these columns to be made.

Lion Capital of Ashoka

Commissioned by Ashoka and created from a single block of sandstone, the Lion Capital of Ashoka is a sculpture of **FOUR ASIATIC LIONS** standing back to back. Each lion has its mouth open and they face the four cardinal directions (north, east, south and west) to symbolise the **SPREADING OF BUDDHIST TEACHINGS** across the land.

Palm-leaf manuscripts

Lists of herbs and plants used as **REMEDIES** were written on pressed palm-tree paper. One list referred to 'medicinal herbs, roots and fruit, whether useful to man or to beast, have been brought and planted wherever they did not grow', which tells us that Ashoka made sure both people and animals had **ACCESS TO MEDICINE**.

ASHOKA'S LEGACY

During the eighth year of Ashoka's reign, and before he discovered Buddhism, he conquered the Kingdom of Kalinga which claimed the lives of nearly a hundred thousand people. It was a horrific event, and one that made him change his ways. Over the years that followed he studied and started spreading the teachings of Buddha, but after his death in 232 BCE the empire fell under new rule, and his messages of tolerance and compassion were lost.

Edicts

The **WELFARE OF ANIMALS** was just as important to Ashoka as the care of humans. Stone pillars and rocks were inscribed with Ashoka's edicts – passages of text reminding people how to live compassionately with each other. By embracing Buddhism, Ashoka proposed the first animal-rights laws in India: *Here no living being must be killed and sacrificed.*

Edicts are among the first examples of writing in Indian history. They were not carved in Sanskrit, the official state language, but in local dialects. This was so the messages could be more widely understood. Some of Ashoka's edicts were inscribed in Brahmi and Kharosthi, languages which became extinct in the fifth century CE. For millennia, the edicts' true meaning were unknown until nineteenth-century archaeologists discovered coins with Brahmi and Kharosthi characters. They deciphered entire scripts of Ashoka's words and the beliefs of his kingdom were finally understood.

Dams

Ashoka believed the state should provide for its people, and so he built facilities for the people of the Mauryan Empire. Dams made of **INTERLOCKING SANDSTONE BLOCKS** allowed for huge volumes of clean water to be accessible for all. Each dam was connected to Buddhist monasteries that managed and **DISTRIBUTED WATER FAIRLY** among residents, feeding an entire village from one river and creating reservoirs for larger towns and cities.

Writings, buildings and shrines were damaged when invaders attacked India 1,400 years later, impacting our knowledge of Ashoka's contribution to early Buddhism. Since the twentieth century, excavations at Ashokan cities and Buddhist centres like Sarnath have shown us how the average person's life was changed for the better because of Ashoka, which has led to this great Mauryan emperor being placed back into the heart of India's early history.

ANCIENT MAKAH LIVED IN HARMONY WITH NATURE

WHEN
Around 200 CE

WHERE
Ozette, USA

The Makah are known as people of the sea and forest.

About two thousand years ago, the Makah could be found along the Pacific Northwest coast of the modern United States, living in harmony with nature. Ozette was the largest of five main Makah villages, and there lived the 'Kwih-dich-chuh-ahtx', as they called themselves, or 'people who live by the rocks and seagulls'. This was their name because their livelihood came from the nature that surrounded their home. Canoes were made from forest materials like red cedar wood and food was found in the water. The Makah were creative about how to use different natural resources and embraced this knowledge in their everyday life. And although a mudslide engulfed several longhouses at Ozette around five hundred years ago, the Makah continued life in their traditional territory, and still remain connected with the natural world today.

Much of what is known about the Makah's natural living is derived from their oral tradition. **SONGS** and **DANCES** were an important way for the Makah to communicate.

The Makah were skilled woodworkers and created **CEREMONIAL MASKS** from western red cedar, alder, yew and spruce. The carvings also told a story, and these tales were passed down the family.

Using **NATURAL RESOURCES** from the forest, the Makah built canoes which took to the water in the hunt for whales, seals and fish.

Back on land, elders had the responsibility of teaching the rest of the group how to use many parts of each animal to **MINIMISE WASTE**.

The Makah respected the plants which sustained them. Stories were told about the great **WESTERN RED CEDAR TREE** that provided material for houses and canoes, as well as the trees, plants and grasses that supplied fibres for baskets and clothes.

THE OBJECTS THAT REVEAL THE Makah's STORY

Canoes

These handmade miniature canoes are exact replicas of the **LIFE-SIZE VESSELS** that were once used by the Makah. They built various sizes, from smaller practice canoes for children to larger 10-metre whaling canoes. For the Makah, living on the water was just as important as living on the land. They would take to the seas as **SKILLED MARINERS**, paddling hundreds of miles to fish and hunt.

In 1969, a total of 361 canoe paddles and 14 canoe fragments were discovered alongside thousands of fishing and hunting artefacts.

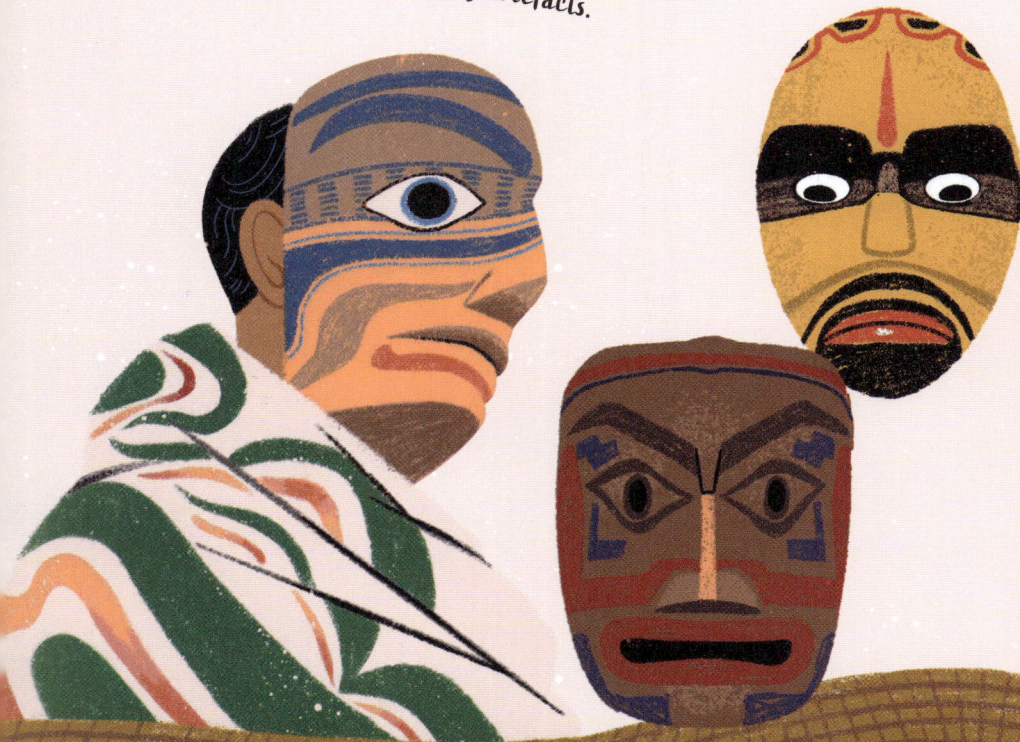

Masks

Intricately carved out of **LOCAL CEDAR** and painted with **NATURAL PIGMENTS** sourced from plants, these masks were worn during important ceremonies. The Makah would communicate the adventures of their ancestors through **SONG** and **DANCE**. Families had the rights to certain dances passed down through the generations, allowing them to share their personal history with other groups.

ABANDONED BUT NOT FORGOTTEN

According to radiocarbon dating, we know that a shift in the land caused a mudslide to swallow Ozette approximately five hundred years ago. For centuries, stories were passed down about a 'great slide' at Ozette, and finally a 1969 storm revealed the historic site. An eleven-year excavation began, producing over fifty-five thousand artefacts, which confirmed the Makah's spoken history to be true.

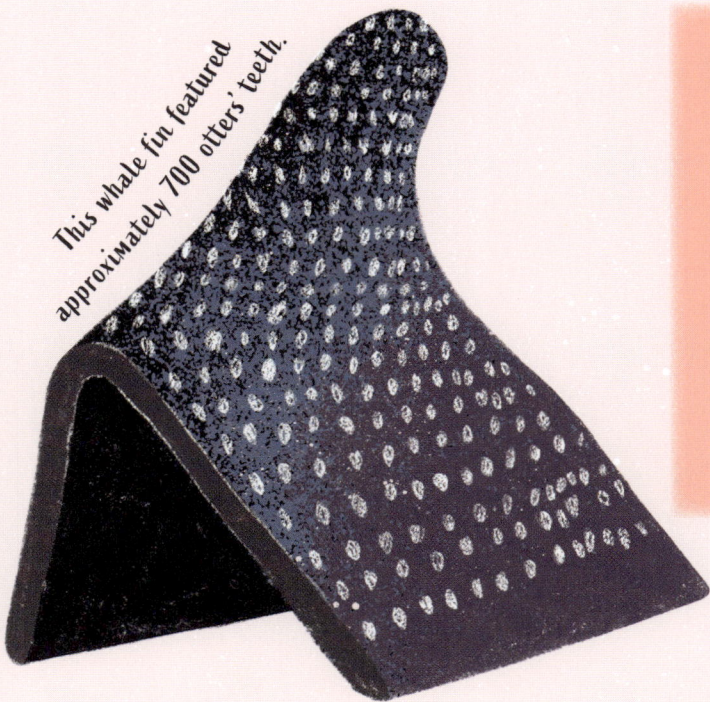

Whale fin

The Makah have a deep connection with nature. This was represented in the art that they made, whether created for a specific ceremony or as an everyday item. A large, I-metre-high whale-fin **EFFIGY** was carved from several pieces of red cedar wood and decorated with otters' teeth. The teeth form the outline of the **THUNDERBIRD**, a powerful, mythical creature in the form of a bird which created rain to encourage vegetation to grow.

Although several houses at Ozette were destroyed by the metres of mud that buried them, the action of the mudslide preserved it in their entirety. Sealed by muddy deposits, oxygen was unable to form which prevented decay, so when archaeologists were invited by the Makah to excavate, organic materials like bark and wood remained intact, as did animal bone, antler and stone tools.

Baskets

Most of the patterns found in baskets were **ANCIENT WEAVING TECHNIQUES** that are still used today. During drier months, the Makah would collect fibres from trees, plants and grasses, and begin a process of picking, drying, folding and storing. In the winter they would begin weaving. **EVERYDAY ITEMS** from combs to stones were stored in these baskets, providing a rare glimpse into the life lived here at Ozette.

Four thousand items of basketry were excavated at Ozette.

These perfectly preserved artefacts are currently housed in a museum in Neah Bay, Washington State, created under the leadership of Edward Eugene Claplanhoo, a Makah elder and former chairman of the Makah Tribe. The museum opened in 1979, a decade after the Ozette site was unearthed. Here, the items that were once buried are now on display to teach others about the Makah's incredible culture and history which is still alive today.

AMERICAN INDIANS LIVED IN COSMOPOLITAN CITIES

The Mississippians thrived in the vibrant city of Cahokia.

Cahokia was a major city that existed near what is now St Louis, Missouri, and it was home to one of the most advanced civilisations in ancient America: the Mississippians. If you took a stroll through it, you would have discovered over a hundred impressive earthen mounds with open plazas, and thousands of houses, temples and public buildings, all organised into complex districts. When this marvel of prehistoric engineering was confirmed as human-made, its history was bypassed in favour of the idea that American Indians were only capable of living in small tribal communities. Yet at its height, Cahokia was the largest and most complex city in the Americas north of Mexico, and in its heyday it rivalled the size of cities like medieval London and Paris.

To the west of Monks Mound, red painted posts were placed in a concentric circle and used to mark **SOLSTICES** (the longest and shortest days) and **EQUINOXES** (when day and night are of equal length).

Cahokia was laid out on a specific plan, and in the centre stood a 30-metre-tall, now known as **MONKS MOUND**. It was the largest example of an earthen mound in North America, and was thought to be where Cahokia's political and spiritual leaders met.

The Grand Plaza was often cleared so that people could play a game with stones and spears called **CHUNKEY**. Chunkey was designed to unite the city's people and was so popular that visitors would come to Cahokia to watch competitors play.

Contrary to the perception of American Indians living a nomadic existence, at its peak Cahokia was home to up to **20,000 CITIZENS**.

Like city-dwellers in other parts of the world, the Mississippians enjoyed a party. Festivals at Cahokia were mostly centered around **GREAT FEASTS**.

THE OBJECTS THAT REVEAL Cahokia's STORY

Stone hoe

The **STONE HOE** was a key tool in the Mississippian culture and reveals the ambitious construction industry at the heart of this metropolis. The tool was formed from sharp blades slotted into wooden handles and was fixed by winding strips of animal hide to bind the blade and secure it into place. Tonnes of soil were excavated with chert hoes to create the 120 **EARTHEN MOUNDS** that covered Cahokia's city centre.

As well as for building vast earthen mound complexes, stone hoes were used for digging up crops to feed the city's large population.

Woodhenge

One of the most dramatic discoveries was that the Mississippians were **ASTRONOMERS**. Woodhenge was a circle made up of **LARGE WOODEN TIMBER POSTS**; it was built several times during the history of the Mississippian people so it must have held some significance. The posts were also painted using red ochre, a natural earth pigment which was believed to have spiritual value, further suggesting the importance of the Cahokia Woodhenge.

A LASTING LEGACY

Cahokia continued as a thriving metropolis until 1350. When European colonisers set foot on American soil a few centuries later, they could not believe that American Indians were sophisticated enough to build or prosper in a city like Cahokia. But excavations unearthed towering structures that rose above the landscape – their construction vast and impressive, large enough to rival any European city at the time.

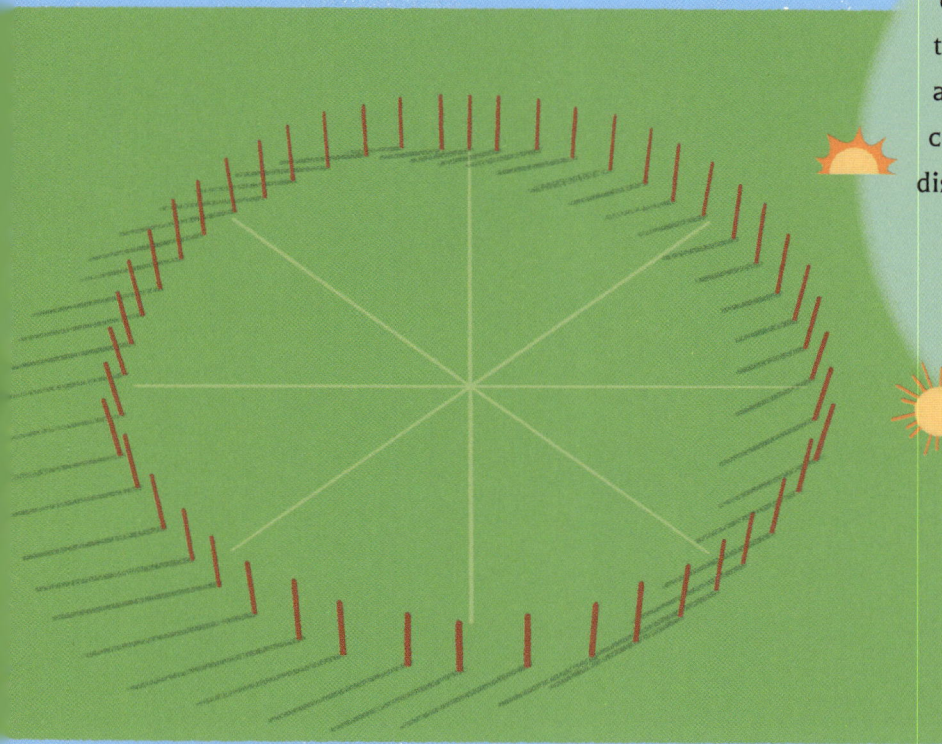

Archaeologists drew post-holes on a plan and soon realised that the Woodhenge timbers were purposely placed, evenly spaced out and grouped together to create a circle. They then compared this to the sun's annual movements and discovered that the wooden circle was being used as a giant sundial – but instead of telling the time, the rising sun cast its rays on different posts as the seasons changed, thereby telling the Mississippians whether it was spring, summer, autumn or winter!

Chunkey player

This clay figure depicts a **CHUNKEY PLAYER**, a participant in a game that originated in Cahokia. Expertly levelled using **SOPHISTICATED ENGINEERING**, the playing area at the Grand Plaza covered 50 acres in total. Disc-shaped stones were rolled across the ground and players would throw spears where they thought the stones would come to a stop. This required good judgement, skill and a precise aim!

Chunkey was designed to bring people of the region together, from the city's farmers to tourists.

After reaching its population height by about 1100, the population of Cahokia shrunk and by 1350 it had largely disappeared. Archaeologists are still trying to understand why this happened: some believe it was due to an environmental disaster; others suggest a political clash with a neighbouring group. One thing they're all certain about is that over a thousnad years ago, the Mississippians foreshadowed the American cities we know and live in today.

THE VIKINGS WERE ALSO PEACEFUL TRADERS

WHEN
Around 960 CE

WHERE
Hedeby,
Germany

Hedeby was a thriving Viking port town that welcomed traders from around the world.

Ask someone to describe the Vikings and chances are they will talk about white people with blond hair who pillaged as their only way of living. But at Hedeby we discover a hidden history... Vikings were actually multicultural, and their towns were filled with skilled craftspeople and resourceful traders. For the Vikings who left their homeland and took to the sea, many settled peaceably in new places. They shared technology, swapped ideas and often lived side by side in harmony with their contemporaries. This was the case some thousand years ago, as a small town known as Hedeby became an important Viking trading centre, home to a 'melting pot' of diverse ideas and cultures.

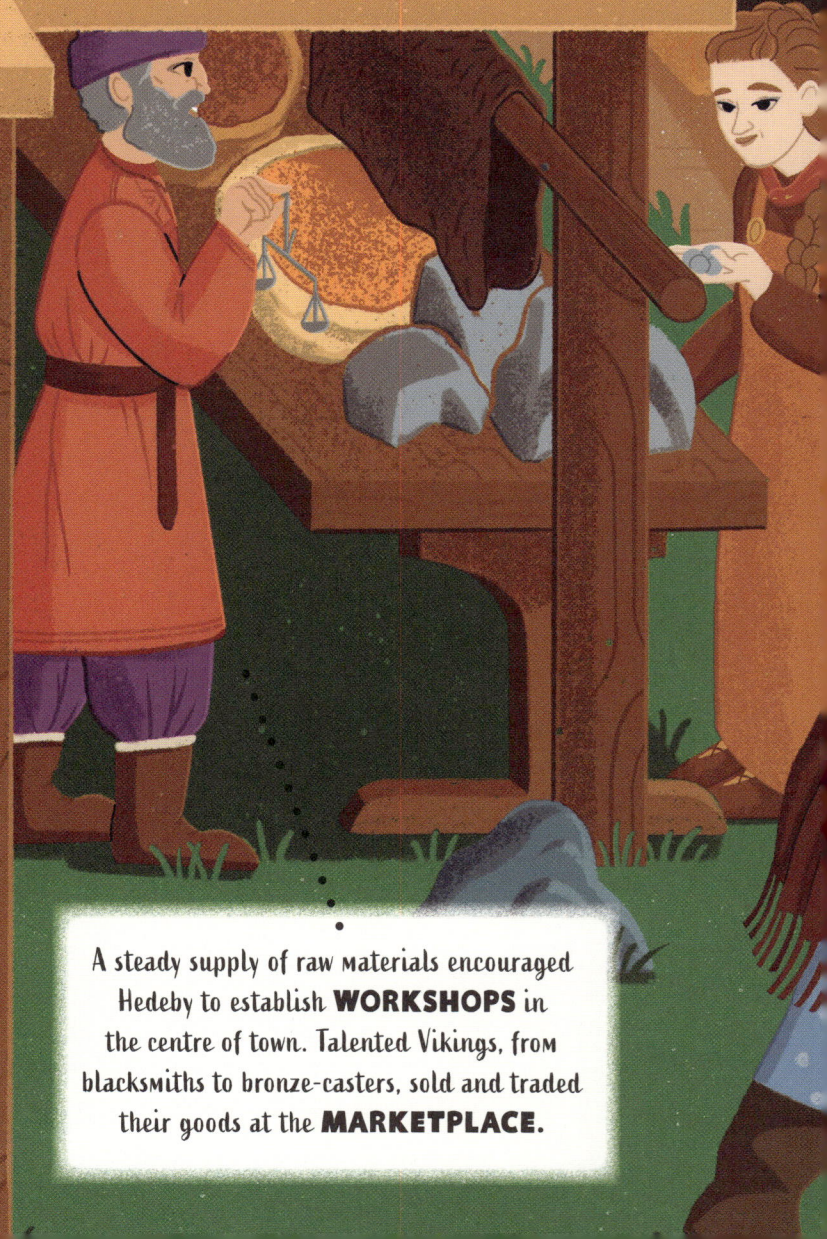

A steady supply of raw materials encouraged Hedeby to establish **WORKSHOPS** in the centre of town. Talented Vikings, from blacksmiths to bronze-casters, sold and traded their goods at the **MARKETPLACE**.

Forty-metre **VIKING LONGSHIPS** navigated the waters of the world. Powered by wooden oars and strong sails, they carried **AMBER** from the **BALTICS**, **SOAPSTONE** from the **SHETLAND ISLANDS** and **GRAIN** from **FRANCE**.

Hedeby was strategically located near **TRADE ROUTES** and well connected to the Baltic Sea so that traders could come and go as they pleased.

Silver was the most precious metal of the Viking Age. At Hedeby the Vikings adopted the use of silver coins, known as **DIRHAMS**, to entice foreign traders to visit their markets... and it worked! **AL-TARTUSHI**, a prominent merchant, paid Hedeby a visit and later told the world about it in an extract from his diary.

THE OBJECTS THAT REVEAL Hedeby's STORY

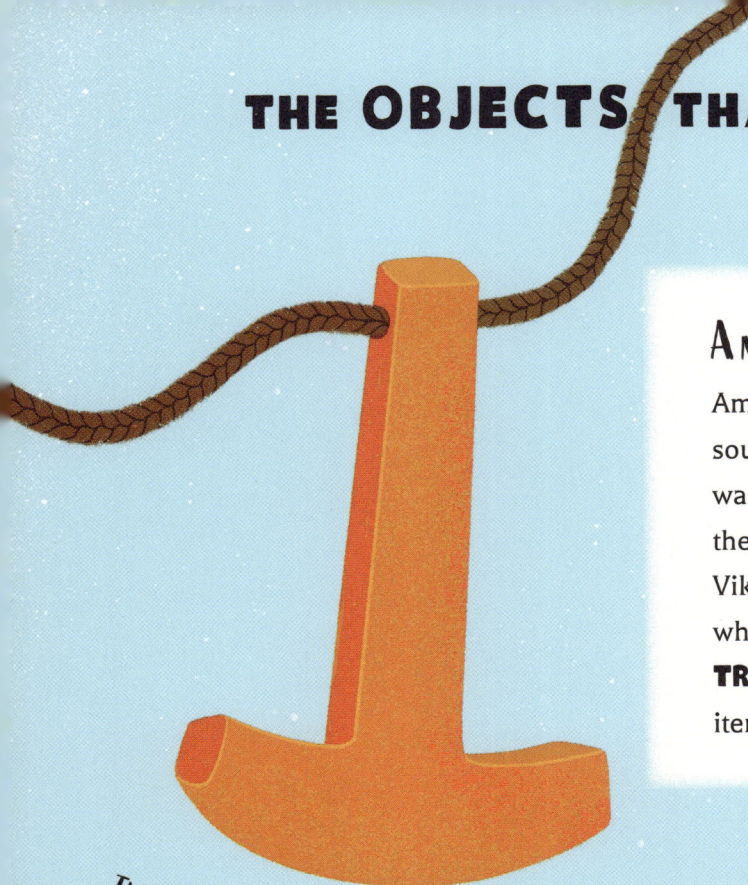

Amber pendant

Amber was sourced around the **BALTIC SEA** and was highly sought-after across empires. Traditionally, this **GEMSTONE** was traded over land along the 'amber road' (a route that linked the shores of the Baltic to Greece, Turkey and Rome), but the Vikings used their **LONGBOATS** effectively to navigate seas which cut down the time that amber took to reach **FOREIGN TRADING PORTS** like Hedeby. The amber was used to create items such as beads and fine jewellery in the town's workshops.

This hammer-shaped amber pendant was typically worn around the neck, either attached to a silver chain or threaded onto a piece of leather.

Dirhams

Thousands of **SILVER COINS**, known as dirhams, were exchanged at Hedeby's marketplace. These coins were accepted as currency and passed through merchants' hands **ALONG TRADE ROUTES**, moving out of the Middle East into central Asia, eventually making their way to northern Europe ports and towns like Hedeby. Using a set of scales and weights, the number of silver coins needed to complete a deal could be precisely worked out – making trade quick and easy.

Arabic inscriptions cover both faces of dirhams and, just like our coins today, they tell us where they originated from and the date they were minted.

FIERCE INVADERS OR CLEVER TRADERS?

For hundreds of years, Hedeby grew in wealth due to its prized location, but it proved all too tempting for rival rulers who fought for its ultimate control. In 1066, the town was invaded, sacked and burned by a Slavic army, resulting in Hedeby's 2,000 residents being forced to relocate to other towns across the Viking world.

Al-Tartushi's diary

Hedeby was the **'GO-TO' DESTINATION** for traders. We know this because Al-Tartushi, a tenth-century Hispano-Arabic, Sephardi Jewish merchant, travelled from his hometown in Al-Andalus, now modern Córdoba, Spain, to Hedeby to experience other **CULTURES** and **ECONOMIES**. During this time, he kept a diary and described what he learned on his travels, calling Hedeby 'a large town at the extreme end of the world ocean'.

Al-Tartushi's diary gives us a unique insight into life at Hedeby and what the Vikings were really like. He paints a vivid picture of the port town, sharing what the Vikings wore, ate and even how they sang! We know he was impressed by the make-up that both men and women wore, but not by their singing, as he wrote, 'Never did I hear singing fouler than that of these people, it is a rumbling emanating from their throats, similar to that of a dog but even more bestial!'

For over a thousand years, nobody knew that the Vikings were clever merchants proficient at trade. When archaeologists began to excavate at Hedeby in 1900, they uncovered the true story. To date, only 5 per cent of the site has been excavated, but through the thousands of objects already recovered, we have gained an insight into the Vikings as people who operated an open society, adopted ideas and welcomed foreigners to live and trade in their port town.

GREAT ZIMBABWE BLASTED COLONIAL IDEOLOGY

WHEN
Around 1000–1590 CE

WHERE
Zimbabwe, Africa

Great Zimbabwe was a medieval stone city of astounding prestige built by the Shona people.

Today, the city of Great Zimbabwe in southern Africa lies in ruins. But a thousand years ago, it was a land full of possibilities: plains of fertile soil to support farming, and mineral resources to provide gold and copper for trading. It was a magnificent place to call home and for the next six centuries Great Zimbabwe operated as an African superpower, dominating trade and commerce in the medieval world. And yet, its history is defined by decades of disputes about who built it. During the European colonisation of Africa, racist historians claimed the ruins couldn't be of African origin; that African people never had the sophistication needed to work gold, trade goods or build a kingdom. How wrong they were...

The Shona are a people whose ancestors built an **IMPRESSIVE STONE CITY**. Great Zimbabwe was divided into three architectural zones: the hill complex, the great enclosure and the valley suburbs.

Birds carved from **SOAPSTONE** stood proudly on guard atop the walls and monoliths of the city's columns. These sculptures are **UNIQUE** to Great Zimbabwe and held great spiritual value for the Shona people.

At its peak, Great Zimbabwe housed around 10,000 residents, suggesting that the Shona people's longevity was likely based on maintaining a **GOOD ECOLOGICAL BALANCE** between population and available resources.

Crafted in expertly-worked stone and fitted without the use of mortar, the walls here curved and flowed thanks to the **ARCHITECTURAL PRECISION** of the Shona people.

Great Zimbabwe was part of a **LARGE TRADING NETWORK**. Small, purpose-made crucibles were used for melting local gold and copper, which were exchanged for pottery from China, glass beads from Syria and bronze from Persia.

THE OBJECTS THAT REVEAL Great Zimbabwe's STORY

Conical tower

Within the great enclosure, a spectacular circular tower – 5 metres wide and 11 metres high – was designed and built by hand. Architects and stonemasons used **INGENIOUS METHODS** to construct the buildings of Great Zimbabwe: granite blocks were heated in a fire, and then cold water would be poured over the blocks to crack them into brick-shaped pieces. Millions of these pieces were stacked cleverly without the use of mortar. The function of this tower is unknown, but it is thought that the Shona people stored their **SURPLUS SUPPLIES OF GRAIN** inside.

This structure took over thirty years to complete and demonstrates remarkable skill.

Soapstone birds

When the ruins of Great Zimbabwe were excavated in the late nineteenth century, eight prized **SOAPSTONE SCULPTURES OF AFRICAN FISH EAGLES** were unearthed. Each bird was 40 centimetres tall and sat proudly on top of a column almost a metre tall. It is thought these sculptures once stood in the hill complex, a place where important religious rituals and royal ceremonies took place.

This ancient bird has since been adopted as the symbol of the Zimbabwean people, signifying how the country is reclaiming its history.

A CAUTIONARY TALE

In the late nineteenth century, European colonisers were stunned by Great Zimbabwe's excellence. Blinded by their racism, they did not believe that such a place could have been built by Black Africans. Even after archaeologists found evidence that the Shona people had built Great Zimbabwe, the country's white colonial government tried to discredit it, and even bribed historians to write accounts that disputed the truth.

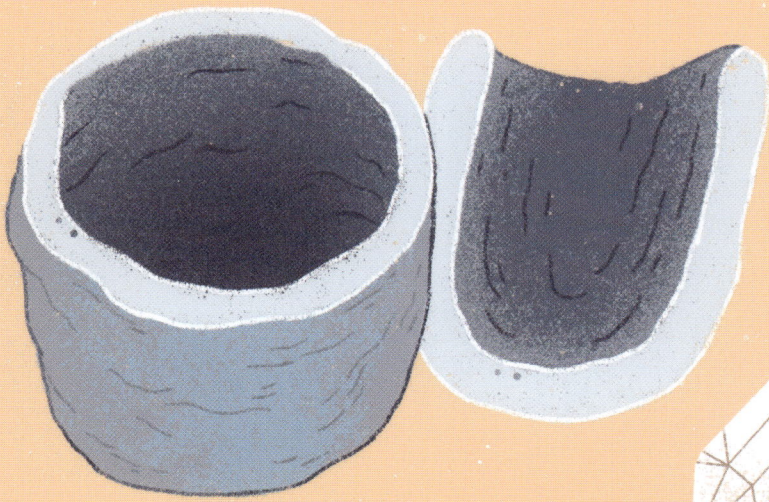

Crucibles

More than a hundred crucibles were discovered at Great Zimbabwe. These small containers were made from the granite-rich clay and used to smelt the precious metals mined there. At least four thousand **GOLD MINES** and five hundred **COPPER MINES** were in operation in Great Zimbabwe, and during the medieval period 40 per cent of the world's total mined gold came from Great Zimbabwe!

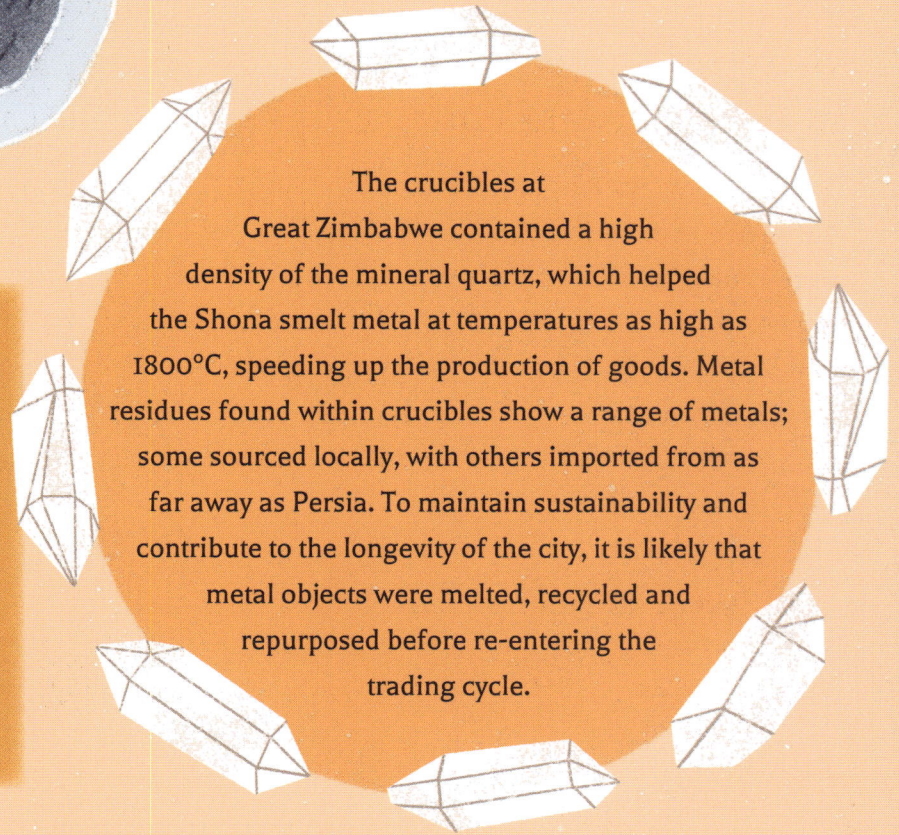

The crucibles at Great Zimbabwe contained a high density of the mineral quartz, which helped the Shona smelt metal at temperatures as high as 1800°C, speeding up the production of goods. Metal residues found within crucibles show a range of metals; some sourced locally, with others imported from as far away as Persia. To maintain sustainability and contribute to the longevity of the city, it is likely that metal objects were melted, recycled and repurposed before re-entering the trading cycle.

Chinese porcelain

Fragments of blue-and-white Chinese porcelain have been dug up. Glued together, the delicate pieces form about a third of a **MING DISH** dating from the sixteenth century. The discovery of such fine and sought-after porcelain highlights the **SOPHISTICATION OF THE TRADE NETWORKS** at Great Zimbabwe. To bring economic stability, the Shona people established extensive commercial and trading networks linking Africa with merchants based around the Indian Ocean.

By the time the truth was exposed, the ruins of Great Zimbabwe had been looted of anything of value, and objects were sold to museums around the world without any context concerning where they were found. As a result, there is still so much to be discovered about life in Great Zimbabwe, and although Africa is the continent in which human life began, we unfortunately know less about African history than anywhere else in the world.

ANCESTORS OF THE INUIT HAD AN EQUAL SOCIETY

WHEN
Around 1200–1600 CE

WHERE
Qilakitsoq,
Greenland

In ancient Inuit communities, each person played a crucial role in the survival of the group.

Around seven hundred years ago, the ancestors of present-day Inuit peoples, known as the Thule, successfully inhabited the Arctic. These communities lived in one of the harshest environments ever known, and the cold climate demanded that they had the right shelter, clothing and tools to keep warm, dry and fed. After all, something as minor as a wet foot could result in frostbite, and perhaps even death! And so, cooperation instead of competition was valued. The best person was chosen to perform each specific role, and the responsibilities faced by Thule women were considered equally as important as those taken on by Thule men.

TATTOOS adorned the faces of Thule women. Each tattoo signified an important accomplishment, from catching a whale to sewing a sealskin parka.

A whole community's survival could be dependent on a family member's **SEWING SKILLS**. Overlapping pieces of an animal's skin were stretched out and sewn together to make waterproof clothes and shoes.

Animals were the primary food source as vegetation rarely grew there. Using tools like toggled harpoons, whales and seals were **HUNTED BY MEN AND WOMEN** on the water, while caribou and snow foxes were captured on land.

The Thule placed a high value on **INCLUSIVENESS**, **RESOURCEFULNESS** and **COLLABORATION**. While family members were expected to fulfil their role in society, everyone also had to play their part in supporting and helping others.

THE OBJECTS THAT REVEAL THE Inuit's ancestors' STORY

Toggle harpoons

Made from a wooden handle and an iron blade, **TOGGLE HARPOONS** helped hunters to capture animals on land and sea with ease. The blade of a toggle harpoon was attached to a sinew rope, but it cleverly detached from the main handle upon entering the animal's body. Thule families would **WORK AS A TEAM** to hunt and then share the spoils fairly – behaviour which was crucial to their **RESILIENCE**.

Qilakitsoq mummies

Eight bodies were unearthed in two graves protected by a rock overhanging by a shallow cave. The discovery of six females and two children revealed that more than 75 per cent of their diet consisted of marine mammals and fish; the rest likely came from reindeer and other game. Furthermore, ultraviolet examination showed that the women's foreheads, eyebrows and chins were **ADORNED WITH TATTOOS** that were made by tapping or poking the skin with a soot-dipped needle.

Men, women and children were buried together and shared the same plot equally.

LIFE ON THE EDGE

The Qilakitsoq settlement was abandoned in the 1800s and the Thule moved to the Arctic regions of Canada, Greenland, Alaska and Russia where they reside today. However, climate change means they're being forced to adapt. Rapidly melting ice now makes travelling and hunting unstable, and the skills learned from older generations may soon become impossible to use in the changing landscape.

Sealskin boots

Soft boots known as kamiks were crafted using a **THOUSAND-YEAR-OLD METHOD**. Each boot was made from overlapping pieces of reindeer skin or sealskin. The pieces were finely stitched together with sinew thread which was fed through tiny holes punched with a bone awl tool. This design created a watertight seal, and each shoe was further insulated with hay and worn over socks to protect the wearer from frostbite. This **CLEVER INNOVATION** enabled feet to remain dry and warm in the freezing-cold Arctic.

We know so much about Thule life because of these eight bodies. You may wonder how we can tell so much from centuries-old bones – it's because these mummies were incredibly well preserved due to the Arctic climate: the cold temperatures coupled with extremely dry air effectively freeze-dried the bodies.

These boots were soft-soled and moved in motion with the feet, which allowed hunters to travel very quietly.

In response, a new field of glacial archaeology is emerging: an attempt to recover the disappearing traces of ancient and historical cultures that once lived on the ice sheets. Thule communities are working with archaeologists to help recover and record evidence of their culture. And as the ice swiftly melts, the race to preserve this way of life becomes more important so we can better understand the incredible ancestors who once lived on the frozen edges of the world.

MACHU PICCHU WAS BUILT ON MIGRATION

WHEN
Around 1450–1530 CE

WHERE
Machu Picchu,
Peru

The story of Machu Picchu is a story of human migration.

Around six hundred years ago, a glorious citadel nestled high in the Andes. Machu Picchu was constructed as a royal estate for Incan emperors, but soon became home to entire communities of skilled workers who moved hundreds of miles to start a new life. In no time they were important members of society, from artisans weaving tunics and farmers managing alpaca herds to record-keepers collecting taxes and engineers designing temples. Their talents were revered by Incan emperors, and they in turn embraced their new lives at Machu Picchu and helped it to prosper for nearly a century.

Hailing from the four corners of the vast Inca Empire, around seven hundred and fifty skilled workers moved to Machu Picchu and were collectively known in society as the **YANAKUNA**.

Terraced fields were built on the mountainside to allow rainwater to run down the steps and feed crops. This **INNOVATIVE DESIGN** provided residents with food, from potatoes and tomatoes to quinoa and maize.

Earthquakes were common at Machu Picchu so the yanakuna constructed buildings with this in mind. Their forward-thinking **MASONRY SKILLS** contributed to loose-fitting stones which bounced during tremors and, instead of falling apart, fell back into position!

The yanakuna designed some of Machu Picchu's **AMAZING ARCHITECTURE**, from palaces to storage buildings. They recorded their progress on their unique writing system: a **QUIPU**.

SKILLED WEAVERS produced **BEAUTIFUL TUNICS** made from alpaca wool. Known for crafting the finest cloth across the Inca Empire, their textiles were more precious than gold or silver.

Cultures across the ancient Andean world used quipus for thousands of years.

Quipu

The Inca had no written language and instead used a quipu, an **INTRICATE SYSTEM** of knotted strings of various colours. A horizontal main cord was looped with coloured vertical threads, tied and knotted to mark the information the user wanted to convey. Not unlike early computers, the quipu was used in lots of different ways: for collecting data, keeping records and monitoring money.

Butterfly plates

Plates were the most popular ceramic item used for serving food and many were beautifully painted with animal patterns. The variety of ceramics discovered at Machu Picchu showed that the people who lived here came from all over the Inca Empire, reflecting the **DIVERSITY OF ITS POPULATION**. Many of these plates were repaired during their lifetime, which indicated their special significance to the yanakuna who owned them. They were even buried with them!

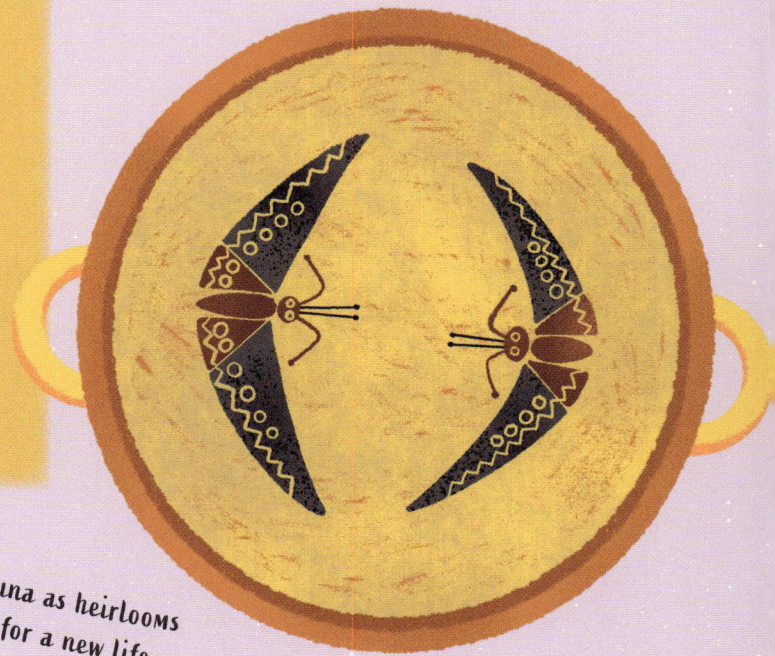

Plates were given to the yanakuna as heirlooms before they left their homes for a new life.

INCAN INSPIRATION

The citadel of Machu Picchu was short-lived, lasting for just under a century. It ended around the same time that the Spanish conquest of the Inca Empire began in 1532, but there's no evidence that Machu Picchu was ever attacked. It is thought most of the yanakuna died of smallpox, an infectious disease that ravaged its population after being introduced by European conquistadors.

Over a hundred and fifty burials were discovered at Machu Picchu. Archaeologists used scientific techniques such as isotope analysis to look at the different types of atoms absorbed in the yanakuna's teeth from the food they ate. When comparing this to skeletal evidence, we know that the people buried at Machu Picchu migrated from all over the Inca Empire, and also that there was an equal split of males and females.

Tunic

Tunics carefully woven with wool combed from alpacas were valuable items. The characters and patterns on the cloth were symbolic, often relating to astronomy. Tunic patterns could also hint at where the weaver was trained, or from which region they came from before relocating to Machu Picchu. The above star pattern is typically from the southern coast of Peru, where the **EIGHT-POINTED STAR** was a common motif. It's therefore likely that the person who weaved this tunic had trained there as a teenager.

For centuries Machu Picchu lay abandoned – until it was rediscovered in 1911 and archaeologists started excavating it in 1912. Ever since, the citadel has been a must-see location for tourists and receives nearly a million visitors every year. Tour operators hire guides from Andean villages with knowledge of the Inca trail, bringing a specialist workforce back to Machu Picchu – just as their Incan predecessors had encouraged centuries before.

ASK AN ARCHAEOLOGIST

So much of archaeology is about asking questions.
Where did people live? What did they wear? How did they eat? Once we know the answers we can begin to understand the past. Here are some responses to questions I often get asked about my work as an archaeologist:

HOW DO YOU KNOW WHERE TO DIG?
A lot of pre-excavation work goes into a dig – we use historical records and technology like lasers and satellite imagery to look for evidence of human activity in a particular place. Sometimes we're called in to dig on sites that are in danger of destruction, or we're asked by communities who want to protect their cultural heritage – and because the work affects those who live in these areas, it's important to involve local people in these excavation projects so they can share their knowledge and experience.

HOW DO OBJECTS GET BURIED IN THE FIRST PLACE?
There are several ways in which objects can become buried. Firstly, through natural processes – winds and floods carry sand, dust and soil, and land them on top of buildings and artefacts. These deposits build up over time, burying the archaeological remains. Sometimes catastrophes, like the mudslide we saw at Ozette, speed up this process.

Secondly, through development. When old towns grew into larger towns and cities, whole streets were often buried under layers of demolition rubble or earth intentionally brought into the towns. This is exactly what happened in London, where Roman streets and buildings were covered under metres of made ground – lost settlements lie hidden right under the capital city today!

Lastly, through the actions of humans. Some people buried valuable stuff like gold and jewellery, precious metals or weapons to protect them and keep them safe.

HOW DO YOU UNEARTH AN OBJECT?
Very carefully! When an object is discovered, the heavy digging stops and archaeologists get out their trowels, brushes…and occasionally even lollipop sticks! Soil, sand and excavated material are sifted to retrieve the article. The object is then numbered, photographed and plotted on a scale plan. Archaeologists like to get as much information about where the item was found on site because context is important.

WHAT IS THE MOST EXCITING OBJECT YOU HAVE FOUND?
A mudbrick from Çatalhöyük (a prehistoric site in Turkey which is featured in this book!). I appreciate that may not sound very exciting, but excavating the mudbrick walls of 9,000-year-old houses was truly mind-blowing. Each individually shaped mudbrick was made by the families that lived there, every single one outlined in the walls built there. Moments like that for an archaeologist are priceless; each brick brought me within touching distance of these early farmers who collaborated to build a place they called home.

WHAT HAPPENS TO THE OBJECTS YOU FIND?

The archaeologists of today record every single object found. We are bound by a set of rules known as a code of ethics, and finds are usually passed to places where everyone can see them, like a museum or archive. In the past, archaeologists were not required to follow these rules, and objects were obtained without consent from the communities to which they belonged. This has prompted modern-day archaeologists to ask questions such as 'who does the past belong to?'

DO ARCHAEOLOGISTS MAKE MISTAKES?

Absolutely! Archaeology is only as good as the archaeologists who interpret it, and there is a need for archaeologists to do less telling and more asking and listening. Unfortunately, early archaeologists did not think this was important and that's why, for decades, some sites such as Great Zimbabwe were misunderstood. Most of the first archaeologists were white European men, and their lived experiences and racial prejudices shaped the questions and answers of their research. Thankfully, we're doing better today – building teams of archaeologists from different walks of life and involving local communities to share information about their land, cultures and ancestors.

WHY DOES ARCHAEOLOGY MATTER TODAY?

Archaeology gives us the tools to examine and explain human behaviour – and by studying the past, we can see how humans dealt with key issues like climate change and gender equality. These are matters we are still talking about today, and we can learn important lessons from previous behaviours – and from past mistakes, too. These experiences help us to shape how we live today and also encourage us to build a better future.

HOW CAN I BECOME AN ARCHAEOLOGIST?

There are lots of different paths to becoming an archaeologist. You can even start on your journey now! You may not realise this, but as soon as you step outside of your home you are immersed in an archaeological landscape. Pay attention to how your street looks – is there a mixture of buildings, old and new? If you visit a local museum or library, they'll have old maps, documents and photographs that can tell you about where you live, how the area has evolved and stories about the people who once lived there. Archaeologists are curious people who are always asking why – so if you're the same then you can become one too!

GLOSSARY

ANCESTOR – a person who was in someone's family in past times.

BARTERING – trading goods and services in exchange for other goods and services, rather than using money.

BUDDHISM – a religion based on the teachings of the Buddha, which means 'enlightened'.

CITADEL – a fortified structure designed to provide protection, usually built on a high place.

CLASS – a group of people in society that has been categorised based on social status.

CLIMATE CHANGE – changes in the Earth's climate, especially the gradual rise in temperature caused by high levels of carbon dioxide and other gases.

COLONIALISM – when a powerful country directly controls less powerful countries and uses their resources to increase its own strength and wealth.

COMMODITY – something that is sold for money.

CONQUISTADOR – a sixteenth-century Spanish conqueror of Central and South America.

CONSERVATION – the act of protecting and preserving Earth's natural resources.

COSMOPOLITAN – a place or society that is full of people from many different countries and cultures.

DAM – a wall that is built across a river in order to stop the water flowing and to make a lake.

DIALECT – a form of a language that is spoken in a particular area.

DIVERSITY – the inclusion in a group or activity of people who are, for example, of different races, genders or religions.

EDICT – a command or instruction given by someone in authority.

EFFIGY – a sculpture or model of a person.

EPIGRAPHY – the study of ancient inscriptions.

EQUALITY – the same status, rights and responsibilities for all members of a society, group or family.

GENDER – the characteristics of women, men, girls and boys that are socially constructed; it varies from society to society and can change over time.

HERBIVORE – an animal that only eats plants.

HUNTER-GATHERER – a person who lived by hunting and collecting food rather than by farming.

IDEOLOGY – a particular set of ideas and beliefs.

INCLUSIVITY – the fact of including all types of people, things or ideas, and treating them all fairly and equally.

INSCRIPTION – writing carved into something made of stone or metal.

LOOT – to steal something from a place or person, usually during a war or riot.

MASONRY – the bricks and pieces of stone that are used to make a building.

MELTING POT – a place or situation in which people or ideas of different kinds gradually get mixed together.

METROPOLIS – the largest, busiest and most important city in a country or region.

MIGRATE – to move from one place to another.

MINING – the activities connected with getting valuable or useful minerals from the ground; for example, gold.

MULTICULTURAL – consisting of or relating to people of many different nationalities and cultures.

NOMADIC – travelling from place to place rather than living in one location all the time.

ORAL HISTORY – spoken memories, stories and songs, and the study of these, as a way of communicating and discovering information about the past.

PAGAN – a person whose beliefs and activities do not belong to any of the main religions of the world.

PILGRIMAGE – a long journey to a holy place for a religious reason.

PREJUDICE – an unfair and unreasonable opinion or feeling, especially when formed without enough thought or knowledge.

RACISM – the belief that people of some races are inferior to others, and the negative behaviour which is the result of this belief.

SUPERPOWER – a very powerful and influential country.

SUSTAINABILITY – the ability to exist and develop without destroying natural resources.

TRADING – the act of buying and selling goods and services.